The Cradle
and
The Cross

David E. Owen

The Cradle and The Cross

Unless otherwise indicated, all Scripture quotations are from The King James Version of the Holy Bible (KJV).

Published in the United States of America

Contents

Preface

Conclusion

Preface

As we study the events and details surrounding Jesus' birth, we realize that there is a great deal of suggestion found in the elements of His birth scene.

For example, the fact that there was no room for them in the inn suggests that "He came unto His own, and His own received Him not" (John 1:11). The fact that he was placed in a feeding trough suggests that we can partake of Him as "the bread of life" (John 6:35).

But perhaps more than anything, the aspects of His birth suggest the aspects of His death.

We cannot build doctrine upon shadows and types, but we know that Jesus in a unique sense was, as songwriter Ron Hamilton wrote, "Born to die upon Calvary." And even in His birth we see the shadow of His death. The cradle of Christmas points to the cross of Calvary. Let's consider the comparisons...

Chapter One

The Places Involved In Jesus' Birth and Death

There are many similarities to be found as you study Jesus' birth and His death. We immediately see a foundational comparison between these two events, for in Luke 2:6-7, "the days were accomplished that she should be **delivered**. And she brought forth her firstborn son." We know then that His mother delivered Him in birth. But we also know that His Father delivered Him in death, for the Bible mentions "He that spared not his own Son, but **delivered** him up for us all" (Romans 8:32).

Where did these events take place for Jesus? Are there any similarities between the places where His birth and death occurred?

Years ago, a person's birth and death might both take place in the family home. Now, a person's birth and their death might both occur in a hospital.

As we think about Jesus' birth and death, we learn that these events were neither in a home or a hospital.

We know that Jesus was born in Bethlehem. We also know from Luke 2:7 that He was not born in the inn at Bethlehem. So where specifically was He born? The New Testament doesn't tell us, but the Old Testament does.

The Bible says in Micah 4:8, "And thou, O tower of the flock, the strong hold of the daughter of Zion, unto thee shall it come, even the first dominion; the kingdom shall come to the daughter of Jerusalem."

The phrase "tower of the flock" is the Hebrew phrase "*Migdal Edar*." It is a phrase that is first used in Genesis 35 when Jacob, after burying Rachel at Bethlehem, "journeyed, and spread his tent beyond the tower of Edar" (Genesis 35:21), or the tower of the flock.

In ancient times this tower, which was situated on the outskirts of Bethlehem, was used as a military watchtower, or as Micah said, "a strong hold," in the protection of the area. And throughout the year, it was close to this tower that shepherds kept a particular flock of sheep designated as temple sacrifices. The shepherds would bring the ewes into the sheltered area beneath the tower where they would give birth to the lambs. The shepherds would inspect the lambs to make sure they were without spot or blemish, and to make sure they would be acceptable sacrifices at the temple at Jerusalem at some point. Sometimes the shepherds would swaddle the newborn lambs, wrapping their little legs in bands of cloth to protect their weak limbs.

Micah indicated that the ruler and the king would come to the tower of the flock; therefore it's very possible that Jesus' birth could have taken place at this tower, close to those shepherds and their flock.

I believe that Jesus was born at this tower just outside of Bethlehem, and I know that He died on a tree just outside of Jerusalem.

Bethlehem lies roughly six miles to the southwest of Jerusalem, and the events of Jesus' birth and death were separated by a span of 33 years. Yet we discover a fascinating intersection of thought between these two locations.

In Both Places, We See the Overwhelming Crowd

The Bible tells us "there was no room for them in the inn" (vs. 7). Because of the taxation or census of Augustus, Bethlehem would have been filled well beyond capacity. And while hospitality was, according to some writers, a key element of Jewish life, the homes and private guest chambers had all been filled long before the arrival of Joseph and Mary. Thirty-three years after his birth, the Bible mentions a "multitude" in Jerusalem (Luke 23:1), and then we are told that as Jesus was led to Calvary "there followed him a great company of people" (Luke 23:27). Thirty-three years earlier a *census* had gathered a crowd. Now, 33 years later, a *crucifixion* had gathered a crowd. We might also contrast the "multitude of *the heavenly host*" that wanted to glorify Him in Luke 2:13 with the multitude of *the hateful host* that wanted to "Crucify Him" in Luke 23:21.

In Both Places, We See Outside the Camp

The Greek word for "inn" in Luke 2:7 implies some type of simple building of varying size known as a *khan* or a *kataluma*, and these would offer the traveler the protection of walls and a roof, and water, but little more. According to the 19th century preacher and writer Cunningham Geikie, the inn would often consist of a rectangular outer perimeter of rooms surrounding an open square. If this was the case in Bethlehem, then they were forced to go outside of the rectangular, enclosed area of the inn to accommodate the birth of Jesus. Just as there was no place to receive Him in birth, there was no pardon to release him from death. For "they cried, saying, Crucify him, crucify him" (Luke 23:21). And the Bible tells us that Jesus, in order "that He might sanctify the people with His own blood, suffered without the gate" (Hebrews 13:12). Just as they had gone outside of the rectangular, enclosed inn for his birth – they had gone outside the walls of the city of Jerusalem for his death.

In Both Places, We See the Overshadowed Circumstances

As darkness crept across the Judean hills and valleys around Bethlehem, Mary began to experience the pain and sorrow of childbirth as "she brought forth her firstborn son" (vs. 7). Jesus would later speak of the pains of childbirth when He said, "A woman when she is in travail hath sorrow, because her hour is come: but as soon as she is delivered of the child, she remembereth no more the anguish, for joy that a man is born into the world" (John 16:21). He essentially said that in the process of birth, joy follows sorrow. And His particular birth brought joy, not just to a woman, but joy to a world.

Similarly, at the time of Jesus' death in Jerusalem, the Bible says that "there was darkness over the whole land" (Mark 15:33). And "Jesus ... for the joy that was set before Him endured the cross, despising the shame, and is set down at the right hand of the throne of God" (Hebrews 12:2). He knew that in the process of His death upon the cross, joy would follow sorrow.

Chapter Two

The Personalities Involved In Jesus' Birth and Death

To read of the Nativity of Christ and the Passion of Christ is to become acquainted with a number of individuals. The *categorical diversity of the sexes* is not a limitation, for in both of these wonderful events, we find the involvement of both men and women. The *cosmological diversity of spheres* is not an issue, for we find the inclusion of both human beings and heavenly beings.

There Are Those Who Have A Close Involvement in These Events

After His birth, two individuals were closely present — a man named Joseph and a woman named Mary. Perhaps it was Joseph that "wrapped Him in swaddling clothes, and laid Him in a manger" (Luke 2:7) as Mary looked on. Correspondingly, after His death, three were closely present — a man named Joseph and two women named Mary. Mark tells us that Joseph of Arimathaea "bought fine linen, and took Him (Jesus) down, and wrapped Him in the linen, and laid Him in a sepulchre which was hewn out of a rock, and rolled a stone unto the door of the sepulchre. And Mary Magdalene and Mary the mother of Joses beheld where He was laid" (Mark 15:46-47).

There Are Those Who Have A Connected Involvement in These Events

It still thrills my heart to hear of *the abiding watchmen*, these shepherds, who were "abiding in the field, keeping watch over their flock by night" (Luke 2:8). Every shepherd may have been "an abomination unto the Egyptians" (Genesis 46:34), but these particular shepherds have had the privilege of being indelibly connected to the herald angel who announced the birth and visitation of the Divine One. But in like manner, we also see *the attending women* who, "when the sabbath was past ... had bought sweet spices, that they might come and anoint" Jesus after His death (Mark 16:1). "And entering into the sepulchre, they saw a young man sitting on the right side, clothed in a long white garment" (Mark 16:5). And it is here that we find their connection to the angel who announced the victory of the dead One Who was now risen.

There Are Those Who Have A Comforting Involvement in These Events

In the time following the birth of Jesus, when the angel of the Lord interrupted the stillness and silence of night, the Bible says that the shepherds "were sore afraid" (Luke 2:9). But then we're informed of the comforting words of this celestial being who said, "Fear not" (Luke 2:10). What a comfort to know that a Saviour is born (as we read in Luke 2:11), that He has come forth from the womb! Likewise, in the days following the death of Jesus, We again find an angel making a comforting announcement to some very frightened people. We might even say that these women were "sore afraid" as they saw this whitely robed young man. But "he saith unto them, Be not affrighted" (Mark 16:6). In other words, "Fear not." What a comfort to know that "He is risen" (Mark 16:6), that He had come forth from the tomb!

Chapter Three

The Particulars Involved In Jesus' Birth and Death

The French novelist Gustave Flaubert said, "God is in the details." I do not dispute this. In fact, as we continue to observe these striking comparisons between the birth and death of the Lord Jesus, the more I am convinced that there was Divine design in all of these details. It seems increasingly clear that the Blessed Babe of Bethlehem was meant to be the Crucified Christ of Calvary. It seems increasingly certain that Jesus was born to die.

Thus far, we have found resemblances between **the places** involved in Jesus' birth and His death. We have found parallels between **the people** involved in His birth and the people involved in His death. As we continue to look at His birth and death, let's consider a few particulars that are similar.

Let's Notice the Particular Clothes in These Two Situations

The Bible tells us in Luke 2:7 that Mary "brought forth her firstborn son," and perhaps Joseph assisted by wrapping the baby "in swaddling clothes." In his book on Bible manners and customs, James Freeman described the swaddling process saying:

> "They tightly wrapped His body and limbs in these broad strips of common cloth to protect the baby's weak limbs. Miss Rogers, an English lady (who had traveled extensively in Palestine), describes the appearance of an infant thus bandaged: 'The infant I held in my arms was so bound in swaddling-clothes that it was perfectly firm and solid, and looked like a mummy'."

In the same fashion, after his death, Joseph of Arimathaea "bought fine linen, and took

(Jesus) down, and wrapped Him in the linen" (Mark 15:46). No doubt, the body was so wrapped "that it was perfectly firm and solid, and looked like a mummy."

Let's Notice the Particular Cots in These Two Situations

At the time of His birth, Jesus was laid in a crib. And I use the term "crib" in both senses of the word — both a baby's bed and a feeding trough. We see Him laid in this "manger" (Luke 2:7), which was thought by some to be a hewn-out or hollowed-out piece of rock. James Freeman indicated that archaeologists discovered mangers in the region that were "cut out of limestone and were approximately three feet long, eighteen inches wide, and two feet deep."

Just as He was laid in a hollowed out stone *crib* after His birth, He was laid in a hollowed out stone *crypt* after His death. For the Bible tells us in Mark 15:46 that Joseph of Arimathaea "laid him in a sepulchre which was hewn out of a rock." And in all likelihood, the stone slab inside this hollowed out rock also had a length twice the measure of the width.

All of these comparisons cannot be mere coincidence. I say again that it points us to the fact that He was born to die!

Let's Notice the Particular Contrast in These Two Situations

As intriguing as the comparisons are between His birth and His death, the truly inspiring element in all of this is seen in a point of contrast. After the birth of Christ, the angel came and said to the scared shepherds, "Fear not … Ye shall find the babe wrapped in swaddling clothes, lying in a manger" (Luke 2:10, 12). Basically, they were told that if they looked in that hollowed out piece of rock, they would find the Saviour.

But here's the critical and notable difference. Three days after the death of Christ, the angel came and said to the worried women, "Fear not ye: for I know that ye seek Jesus, which was crucified. He is not here: for He is risen, as

He said. Come; see the place where the Lord lay" (Matthew 28:5-6). Basically, they were told that if they looked in that hollowed out piece of rock, they would not find the Lord. Why? "For He is risen as He said!"

Truly, He was born to die, but He died to live again, and now He is alive forevermore!

Conclusion

F. W. Farrar wrote, "As the east catches at sunset the colors of the west, so Bethlehem is a prelude to Calvary, and even the infant's cradle is tinged with a crimson reflection from the Redeemer's cross."

Farrar wrote this specifically of the circumcision of Jesus, but as we have observed these numerous comparisons, we realize that it applies to so much more.

As we celebrate Christmas again this year, if you only see the babe of Bethlehem, you've missed out. Jesus is not just a son in a manger. He's the Savior of mankind!

About the Author

Rev. Dr. David E. Owen came to know Christ as Savior when he was eight years old. When he was thirteen years old, he felt that God was calling him to Christian ministry.

A native of Brevard, North Carolina, Dr. Owen has been a contributing writer for sermon periodicals, a teacher in a couple of Bible college settings, and an itinerant evangelist. He has pastored churches in Virginia, North Carolina, and Georgia. Since 2019, he has been a hospice chaplain and pastor in Michigan.

www.ingramcontent.com/pod-product-compliance
Lightning Source LLC
Chambersburg PA
CBHW071805020426
42331CB00008B/2408